T0329294

JOSEPH CONRAD

JÓZEF TEODOR KONRAD NAŁĘCZ KORZENIOWSKI

POLAND'S
ENGLISH GENIUS

JOSEPH CONRAD

JÓZEF TEODOR KONRAD NAŁĘCZ KORZENIOWSKI

POLAND'S
ENGLISH GENIUS

by

M. C. BRADBROOK
Fellow of Girton College

CAMBRIDGE
AT THE UNIVERSITY PRESS
1941

CAMBRIDGE
UNIVERSITY PRESS

University Printing House, Cambridge CB2 8BS, United Kingdom

Published in the United States of America by Cambridge University Press, New York

Cambridge University Press is part of the University of Cambridge.

It furthers the University's mission by disseminating knowledge in the pursuit of
education, learning and research at the highest international levels of excellence.

www.cambridge.org
Information on this title: www.cambridge.org/9781107689244

© Cambridge University Press 1941

First published 1941
First paperback edition 2014

A catalogue record for this publication is available from the British Library

ISBN 978-1-107-68924-4 Paperback

"Être vaincu et ne pas se soumettre est la vraie victoire." PILSUDSKI

CONTENTS

The four quotations which form the Prologue are taken from the Collected Edition of Conrad's works by permission of the publishers, Messrs J. M. Dent & Sons

PROLOGUE

POLAND

THE peasants working in the fields, the great unhedged fields, looked after him from the distance; and sometimes some sympathetic old woman on the threshold of a low, thatched hut was moved to make the sign of the cross in the air behind his back; as though he were one of themselves, a simple village soul struck by a sore affliction....

This countryside where he had been born and spent his happy boyish years—he knew it well—every slight rise crowned with trees among the ploughed fields, every dell concealing a village. The dammed streams made a chain of lakes set in the green meadows. Far away to the north the great Lithuanian forest faced the sun, no higher than a hedge; and to the south, the way to the plains, the vast brown spaces of the earth touched the blue sky....

That country which demands to be loved as no other country has ever been loved, with the mournful affection one bears to the unforgotten dead and with the unextinguishable fire of a hopeless passion which only a living, breathing, warm ideal can kindle in our breasts, for our pride, for our weariness, for our exultation....

PRINCE ROMAN (Tales of Hearsay)

FRANCE

The sky rested lightly on the distant and vaporous
outline of the hills; and the immobility of all things
seemed poised in the air like a gay mirage. On this
tideless sea several tartanes lay becalmed in the
Petite Passe between Porquerolles and Cap Esterel,
yet theirs was not the stillness of death but of light
slumber, the immobility of a smiling enchantment,
of a Mediterranean fair day, breathless sometimes, but
never without life. Whatever enchantment Peyrol
had known in his wanderings it had never been so
remote from all thoughts of strife and death, so full
of smiling security, making all his past appear to
him like a chain of lurid days and sultry nights. He
thought he would never want to get away from it,
as though he had obscurely felt that his old rover's
soul had been always rooted there. Yes, this was the
place for him; not because expediency dictated, but
simply because his instinct of rest had found its home
at last.   *The Rover*

ENGLAND

A week afterwards the *Narcissus* entered the chops of the Channel.

Under white wings she skimmed low over the blue sea like a great tired bird speeding to its nest. The clouds raced with her mastheads; they rose astern enormous and white, soared to the zenith, flew past, and, falling down the wide curve of the sky, seemed to dash headlong into the sea—the clouds swifter than the ship, more free, but without a home. The coast to welcome her stepped out of space into the sunshine. The lofty headlands trod masterfully into the sea; the wide bays smiled in the light; the shadows of homeless clouds ran along the sunny plains, leaped over valleys, without a check darted up the hills, rolled down the slopes; and the sunshine pursued them with patches of running brightness. On the brows of dark cliffs white lighthouses shone in pillars of light. The Channel glittered like a blue mantle shot with gold, and starred by the silver of the capping seas. The *Narcissus* rushed past the headlands and the bays. Outward-bound vessels crossed her track, lying over, and with their masts stripped for a slogging fight with the hard sou'wester. And inshore, a string of smoking steamboats waddled, hugging the coast, like migrating and amphibious monsters, distrustful of the restless waves.

The Nigger of the Narcissus

INSPIRATION

I said "I believe I know what England will do" (this was before the news of the violation of Belgian neutrality arrived), "though I won't tell you, for I am not absolutely certain. But I can tell you what I am absolutely certain of. It is this: If England comes into the war, then no matter who may want to make peace at the end of six months at the cost of right and justice, England will keep on fighting for years, if necessary. You may reckon on that."

"What, even alone?" asked somebody across the room.

I said, "Yes, even alone. But if things go as far as that, England will not be alone."

I think that at that moment I must have been inspired. FIRST NEWS (*Notes on Life and Letters*)

THE MAN

IN the history of English literature there has never been anything like the history of Joseph Conrad; nor, so far as I am aware, has there been anything like him in any other European literature. He was a Pole of the landowning class, who became a Marseilles gun-runner at twenty, an English master mariner at twenty-nine, and one of the great English novelists at thirty-eight. Born in 1857, his childhood was darkened by the savage repressions which Tsarist Russia inflicted on the Poles after the abortive rebellion of 1863. His father, as a leader of the Polish people, was imprisoned and exiled: his mother, who elected to share the exile, was treated with ruthless barbarity and died in 1865. His father, a dying man, returned to Cracow in 1868 and died the next year. He had been a poet, a dramatist, and a translator of Hugo, de Vigny and Shakespeare.

Konrad Korzeniowski was urged to seek his fortune abroad by his guardian and uncle, Tadeusz Bobrowski: but none of the family approved of his plan to be a sailor. However, in 1874, Joseph Conrad went to Marseilles, and here he became engaged in gun traffic for the Carlist party in Spain. Here also he met two people who were to count for more than anything as inspiration to his literature, whose portraits he drew again and again—a lovely Basque girl, whose name is unknown, and Dominic Cervoni, the Corsican sailor.[1] Conrad sailed also to the West Indies and to Istanbul; and it was not until 1878 that he landed at Lowestoft, having joined an English vessel. Till 1894 he sailed in English ships with the one interlude of his Congo adventure in 1890: and though his original romantic impulse had sprung from a reading of Marryat, his efficiency was recognised by the usual certificates from that very unromantic body, the Board of Trade, in 1880, 1883 and 1886, when he took his master's "ticket". The story of his seafaring life is told in his books. He sailed in Australian wool-clippers, traders in Malaya and the Gulf of Siam, and in Mediterranean and home waters. It was only in 1889 that Conrad began his first novel, and not till five years later that he finally gave up the sea. He had a long struggle as an author, for though he was soon recognised by such people as Edward Garnett and Henry James, there was little money in his work, and for nearly twenty years he lived in poverty. Then came prosperity but also the Great War, agonising to Conrad: his son was in the British Army, his feelings triply engaged by his triple fidelity to England, France and Poland. Finally, after a few years of success and ease, he died suddenly in 1924, at the age of sixty-six.

[1] The story is told most directly in *The Arrow of Gold*.

THE WORK

THE veerings of Conrad's reputation would have wakened his sardonic wit. Public favour came when his best work was done; for perhaps twenty years he was one of the most popular authors in England and America. Then his work fell into that shadow which always eclipses the previous generation, the shadow from which Hardy is now emerging. Conrad published his first novel in the year Hardy published his last, the year before the appearance of *A Shropshire Lad*, when the public favourites were Kipling, Rider Haggard and Conan Doyle; an age of romantic pessimism and flamboyant assurance. No period seems more remote than that of the Boer War and the reign of Edward VII, yet it saw the rise of two great writers, Conrad the novelist and Yeats the poet. Both deserve the epithet *majestic*; their power to write of the great simple heroic themes almost frightens the modern reader. It is shocking to find someone handling material that Homer might have used, in language so obviously and opulently beautiful—combining acute arrogant sardonic bitterness with a passionate idealism. Complex themselves, they preferred the plain heroic character,

> ...A mind
> That nobleness made simple like a fire,
> With beauty like a tightened bow, a kind
> That is not natural in an age like this....

Perhaps this unembarrassed grandeur, this tested and fine simplicity emerged because their work was sifted through a civilisation foreign to their own. Yeats, of course, had English as his mother tongue, but his work sprang out of the Irish soil of aristocrats and peasants, heroism and revolt. Conrad's native country was also aristocratic and peasant; but the heroism and revolt were of so much more drastic a kind as to lift the reader straight out of the reign of Edward VII into that of George VI. Whatever else in Conrad has dated, his politics are contemporary. It is easier to understand the following passage in 1941 than it could have been in 1911:

> Nations, it may be, have fashioned their Governments, but the Governments have paid them back in the same coin. It is unthinkable that any young Englishman should find himself in Razumov's situation....He would not have an hereditary and personal knowledge of the means by which an historical autocracy represses ideas, guards its power and defends its existence. By an act of mental extravagance he might imagine himself arbitrarily thrown into prison, but it would never occur to him unless he were delirious (and perhaps not even then) that he could be beaten with whips as a practical measure either of investigation or of punishment.
>
> (*Under Western Eyes*, p. 25)[1]

The whole of that novel shows a "senseless despera-

[1] All references are to the Uniform Edition, J. M. Dent and Sons, 1923–8 (Concord Edition, Doubleday, Page and Co., N.Y.).

tion provoked by senseless tyranny" (p. viii) both
of which to the eyes of the westerner are corrupt
beyond reform.

> There is nothing to reform. There is no legality, there
> are no institutions. There are only arbitrary decrees.
> There is only a handful of cruel—perhaps blind—
> officials against a nation; (p. 133)

while the secret revolutionaries display

> the no less imbecile and atrocious answer of a purely
> Utopian revolutionism, encompassing destruction by the
> first means to hand, in the strange conviction that a
> change of hearts must follow the downfall of any given
> human institution. (p. x)

No wonder the book was unpopular in 1911. It
might have been equally unpopular in 1931, but at
the moment its premises are familiar. Conrad's
political writings are few, but almost without exception they are apt to the present time.

There is, however, more to be said for a revival of
Conrad than such special appeals to current interest.
He is relevant as an artist, both for what he says,
and for what he stands for. From his best work there
springs a sustaining and nourishing force which was
never more serviceable or more needed. He puts
into memorable, vivid, clear formulations those
values, above all those personal values which are
both the weapons and the prizes of the present time.
He is strengthening without being a facile optimist.

No other novelist of this century is at once so solid
and so sensitive; and while much of the literature of
the past decade appears too thin to be read nowa-
days, it is still more fatal for an author to be touched
with complacency. Conrad's subjects are great enough
and his manner is penetrative enough to fit the situation. Perhaps his personal history partly accounts
for the fact. But quite apart from his history, he is
appropriate and he is salutary. In the end he should
stand with Yeats as one of the greatest writers of his
time.

*   *   *   *

The following pages attempt a survey of Conrad's
work. They are partly intended as a guide—for the
novels need sifting. One of Conrad's closest friends
observed:

It does disservice to Conrad to be indiscriminate in
praise of his work.... To lump all his work together, as
if he were always the same Conrad, imperils a just
estimate of his greatness.

(John Galsworthy, "Reminiscences of Conrad", *Castles
in Spain and other Screeds*, Heinemann, 1927, p. 81)

It is also necessary to relate the different novels of
Conrad to each other. One throws light on the next,
as happens with the work of all true writers. A kind
of ordnance map of the Conrad territory is required.
The great "purple patches" have not been brought
out for general edification, because any reader can
gain an immediate pleasure from them, and dis-

cussion serves little purpose. Such a passage as that describing the voyage of the *Narcissus* up-channel, which has been quoted in the Prologue, is popular in the best sense; it can be enjoyed quite simply. Therefore, taking for granted that anyone can enjoy Conrad a little, the aim is to strengthen and deepen that pleasure by showing each part of his work in the light of the whole, and directly increasing the interest of the reader. The purpose is practical, the method analytic; the book is not a substitute for reading Conrad, it does assume that Conrad has been or is to be read. For such a purpose it is natural and proper to follow the chronological sequence of the books, and to look at them in the order in which they were written. One of the difficulties of apprehending Conrad's work is that it changed so much, as he admitted himself ("A Familiar Preface" to *A Personal Record*, p. xxiii). Some of his work has a limited appeal, and some of it is popular and immature. Marked divisions separate his early work from that of his maturity, and his maturity from his relaxed old age. I propose to distinguish the first as "The Wonders of the Deep" (1895–1903), the second as "The Hollow Men" (1904–14), and the third as "Recollections in Tranquillity" (1914–24).[1]

[1] "The Wonders of the Deep", 1895–1903: *Almayer's Folly*, 1895; *An Outcast of the Islands*, 1896; *Tales of Unrest*, 1897 (Karain, The Idiots, An Outpost of Progress, The Lagoon); *The Nigger of the Narcissus*, 1897; *Lord Jim*, 1900; *Youth, a*

The end of the first period is marked not only by a change in subject-matter but also in style. Conrad wrote ironically of his own sense of transition at the time:

...perhaps there never was any change, except in that mysterious, extraneous thing, which has nothing to do with the theories of art: a subtle change in the nature of the inspiration: a phenomenon for which I cannot in any way be held responsible. What however did cause me some concern was that after finishing the last of the stories in the *Typhoon* volume it seemed somehow that there was nothing more in the world to write about.

(Author's Note to *Nostromo*, p. vii)

The third period, whose beginning coincided with the war of 1914, and also with the establishment of

Narrative and two other Stories, 1902 (The Heart of Darkness, The End of the Tether); *Typhoon and other Stories*, 1903 (Falk, Tomorrow, Amy Foster); with F. M. Ford, *Romance*, 1903.

"The Hollow Men", 1904–14: *Nostromo*, 1904; *The Mirror of the Sea*, 1906; *The Secret Agent*, 1907; *A Set of Six*, 1908 (The Informer, Gaspar Ruiz, The Brute, An Anarchist, The Duel, Il Conde); *A Personal Record*, 1909; *Under Western Eyes*, 1911; *Twixt Land and Sea*, 1912 (A Smile of Fortune, The Secret Sharer, Freya of the Seven Isles); *Chance*, 1913; *Within the Tides*, 1915 (The Planter of Malata, The Partner, The Inn of the Two Witches, Because of the Dollars); *Victory*, 1915 (finished, June 1914).

"Recollections in Tranquillity", 1914–24: *The Shadow Line*, 1917; *The Arrow of Gold*, 1919; *The Rescue*, 1920; *The Rover*, 1923; *Suspense* (unfinished), 1925; *Tales of Hearsay*, 1925 (The Warrior Soul, The Tale, The Black Mate, Prince Roman).

Conrad as a public success, is marked by a gap, and
then a return to the more strictly autobiographical
material of his first period; and also by a weakening
or blurring of the style. With the exception of *The
Rover*, Conrad in his last years wrote little which
reached his own highest standards. But the true
nature of these divisions can be made plain only by
a survey of the work itself, when they show themselves as natural groupings with more than a chronological justification.

I. THE WONDERS OF THE DEEP

ALL Conrad's work is based on his personal reminiscences ("More on contacts, and very slight contacts
at that, than on actual experience"—Author's Note
to *Within the Tides*, p. vii). Of perhaps no other author
could it be said that every book he wrote is founded
upon real people and incidents of real life: yet even
the tales of Napoleon include such models from the
life (Peyrol and Attilio, both taken from Dominic
Cervoni: Arlette, taken from the original of Rita de
Lastiola: Lathom, whose very name is unchanged).
In his early period, Conrad did not bother to change
the names of Almayer or Captain Beard of the *Judea*,
and there was much speculation in Malaya on the
identity of the novelist "Conrad", before he was
recognised as "that mate who sailed in the *Vidar*
with Craig".

It would be generally agreed that Conrad's first
three books show promise but not achievement. They
are uneven because he was too close to the experience
he used and also too close to his models. *Almayer's
Folly* was begun on the margins of a copy of *Madame
Bovary*; *An Outcast of the Islands* repeats the
characters and weakly reduplicates the plot of its
predecessor, in the same Malayan scene. Conrad
was to learn from Flaubert only by getting a little
farther away from him. Almayer is not clearly seen,

because he is never presented from the outside:
those few pages given to him in *A Personal Record*
realise him much more precisely. The best parts of
the books are the passages of pure scenic description. After this group of stories Conrad suddenly
found his feet—he had muddled about for some time
with a third long story which was not to be finished
till 1920, when it appeared as *The Rescue*—and wrote
The Nigger of the Narcissus, in which there is neither
a central character, nor a story, and where, though
most of the tale is in the first person plural, he can
take up his own point of view to write it. In *The
Nigger*, Conrad discovered his true field, as in the next
book, *Lord Jim*, he was to discover his method. *The
Nigger* is a celebration and a tribute to the actual
men whom Conrad had known—this is clear from his
letters;[1] and at the end of the tale he allows himself
a brief comment. It is, however, in the recollection
of old Singleton's friends—a passage thrown signi-
ficantly into the past tense—that the theme of the
lyric *conte* is given out first. It is to be "plain heroic
magnitude of mind", seen in terms of the merchant
seaman.

They had been strong as those are strong who know
neither doubts nor hopes. They had been impatient and
enduring, turbulent and devoted, unruly and faithful.

[1] *Life and Letters*, vol. i, p. 165. "I must enshrine my old
chums in a decent edifice." Conrad was Second Mate in the
Narcissus, Bombay to Dunkirk, in 1884.

Well meaning people had tried to represent these men
as whining over every mouthful of their food: as going
about their work in fear of their lives. But in truth they
had been men who knew toil, privation, violence,
debauchery—but knew not fear, and had no desire of
spite in their hearts. Men hard to manage, but easy to
inspire; voiceless men—but men enough to scorn in
their hearts the sentimental voices that bewailed the
hardness of their fate. It was a fate unique and their
own; the capacity to bear it appeared to them the
privilege of the chosen!

(*The Nigger of the Narcissus*, p. 25)

Such a passage is exceptional: the main body of
the work is a rendering of the voyage home, the full
life of the ship, simply in terms of the things seen.
The power of the writing lies in its implications, as
when at the end of the tearing storm scene, the figure
of old Singleton appears immovable above the bat-
tered deck:

He steered with care. (p. 89)

In spite of Conrad's feeling of devotion to his
"chums", he was careful to insist that this was not
a story of the sea.

It gives the psychology of a group of men and renders
certain aspects of nature. But the problem that faces
them is not a problem of the sea, it is merely a problem
that has arisen on board a ship where the conditions of
complete isolation from all land entanglements make it
stand out with a particular force and colouring....My

only sea book and the only tribute to a life which I have
lived in my own particular way is *The Mirror of the Sea*.
                    (*Life and Letters*, vol. II, pp. 341–2)

Though there is perhaps an element of exaggeration—for Conrad grew very tired of being imagined
to "sit here and brood over sea stuff"[1]—this passage
shows that Conrad, in writing about seamen, was not
being merely autobiographical. The sea setting was
a simplification. Conrad, like Wordsworth, chose deliberately the simple character and the simplified life
because "in that condition of life, the elementary
feelings exist in a state of greater simplicity and
consequently may be more accurately contemplated
and more forcibly communicated".[2] The life of a
ship's crew is more unified and more perilous than life
ashore: the material means of safety—those few
sheets of iron between the men and the water—
assume as much importance as any *things* can ever
assume: but they are also peculiarly plastic, alive to
man's power of control. Conrad's ability to fuse the

[1] See R. Curle, *The Last Twelve Years of Joseph Conrad* (Sampson Low, 1928), pp. 41–2: "You know yourself very well that
in the body of my work barely one tenth is what may be called
sea-stuff, and even of that the bulk, that is *Nigger* and *Mirror*,
has a very special purpose, which I emphasize in my preface.
Of course there are seamen in a good many of my books.
That doesn't make them sea stories....I do wish that all those
ships of mine were given a rest."
[2] His immediate model was perhaps *Un Cœur Simple* of
Flaubert.

material and the human, the ship and her crew, into
a single living unit was something that could only
have been learnt at sea; but he has so presented this
unity that it becomes a symbol for all the co-operation
between man and the work of man's hands.

The storm, the death of the Nigger, and his burial
at sea, can all be given in direct statement. The
exactitude of the rendering depends on the fine detail;
and the detail depends very often on simile. Conrad
maintains the exterior method, that is, he describes
only what can be *seen*, but because he describes what
is seen by means of simile, this limitation increases
and concentrates his power of suggestion and implication. The whole scene is dramatised; it is removed
from "realism" by the richness of the similes and
it is tied down to realism by the consistent con-
creteness of the writing; whilst this special kind
of matter of fact treatment is both limited and
intensified to a further degree by the very noticeable
absence of comment:

He spun round *as though he had been tapped on the
shoulder*. He was just in time to see Wait's eyes blaze
up, and go out at once, *like two lamps overturned together
by a sweeping blow. Something resembling a scarlet thread*
hung down his chin out of the corner of his lips—and
he had ceased to breathe.

(*The Nigger of the Narcissus*, p. 155)

The whole tale depends for its richness upon its
limitations. Of this Conrad was aware, as he shows

in the preface. It was a more conscious art than he had shown before.

The artist appeals to that part of our being which is not dependent on wisdom [unlike scientists and thinkers]: to that in us which is a gift and not an acquisition—and therefore more permanently enduring. He speaks to our capacity for delight and wonder, to the sense of mystery surrounding our lives: to our sense of pity, and beauty, and pain....Such an appeal, to be effective, must be an impression conveyed through the senses; and in fact, it cannot be made in any other way, because temperament, whether individual or collective, is not amenable to persuasion. All art therefore appeals primarily to the senses....My task, which I am trying to achieve, is by the power of the written word to make you hear, to make you feel—it is, before all, to make you *see*. That—and no more and it is everything. If I succeed, you shall find there, according to your deserts: encouragement, consolation, fear, charm—all you demand—and perhaps also that glimpse of truth for which you have forgotten to ask....Art itself may be defined as a single-minded attempt to render the highest kind of justice to the visible universe, by bringing to light the truth, manifold and one, underlying its every aspect.

(Author's Preface, pp. viii–x, vii)

Here is Conrad's method as an artist, and here the explanation of his limitation to the world of the senses. Only in such a way can he suggest a unity at once too delicate and too pervasive to be treated by theory or reinforced by emotion. In imitation

of the creed of Razumov, Conrad's Creed may be
given as

> Appearances not Emotions.
> Perceptions not Reflections.
> Dramatization not Discursiveness.
> Suggestion not Statement.
> Implication not Theory.

Conrad disliked handling the emotions even at this
early stage, though later he was to invent subtler
means of dispensing with them. But *The Nigger*, his
first and simplest success, was in some ways his
greatest, in that it is the most "simple, sensuous and
passionate",[1] though Conrad worked on the tale for
six months, in fits of black despair. *The Heart of Darkness* was written in a month and *Youth* in a few days,
and here for the first time appears Marlow.

Conrad's next novel was *Lord Jim*: this work
handles what was to become a main theme in many
of Conrad's stories. In a moment of panic Jim, the
first mate of the *Patna*, abandons his ship—which has
struck a wreck—although she carries 800 passengers.
But the *Patna* does not go down; and Jim's certificate
is cancelled. The story tells of the results. Here it is
clear that a new method must be found. Although
Conrad's plan is still to render concrete appearances,
and to suggest their implications, the core of the

---

[1] This is a description of poetry of course. Conrad cared little
for poetry, except that of Shakespeare and Keats. He was
an enthusiast for Jeremy Taylor.

book is a moral issue, and the issue must be put. Hence the need for Marlow the narrator of the story. The best explanation of Marlow is that of Mr Edward Crankshaw, and it may be summarized as follows.[1]

Marlow's function is to comment. Although a complete character and not a puppet, he shares Conrad's fundamental outlook, and so can speak for him. Comment is necessary since Conrad could not draw a character from the inside; he could not dramatise another man's mind—as for example Browning dramatises all the characters of *The Ring and the Book*, Henry James the characters of *The Awkward Age*, or E. M. Forster some of the characters of *A Passage to India*. That this was a genuine incapacity and not a wanton self-limitation on Conrad's part is proved by the failure of Almayer and—even more disastrous—of Harvey in *The Return*. "He could not invent. He could not see things which were not, or never had been, before his eyes. His whole magnificent perceptiveness depended absolutely on the senses" (*Joseph Conrad*, p. 118).[2] Hence Conrad's reliance on his "contacts". Given the smallest core

[1] Edward Crankshaw, *Joseph Conrad, Some aspects of the art of the novel* (John Lane, The Bodley Head, 1936).
[2] Confirmed by Conrad: "As for the story itself it is true enough in its essentials. The sustained invention of a really telling lie demands a talent which I do not possess." (*Tales of Unrest*: Author's Note, p. vii.)

of fact, he could penetrate, illuminate, fix its signi-
ficance. In *Nostromo* he moved a Mediterranean
sailor to the coast of South America and in *The Rover*
and *Suspense* he puts the same man into the Napo-
leonic period: but he could neither invent a wholly
fantastic character, like Dickens's Mr Pickwick, or
present a character from within, like Mr Joyce's
Stephen Dedalus. "He can look into the depths of
another man's mind. His astounding power of
physical vision enabled him to tell a character from
its external manifestations"[1]. He could read the
weather signs of a man's face. But he could do no
more than put the weather signs down, so selected
that his reader could see them too. Unless he were to
compromise the integrity of the story with a "dear
reader" in Thackeray's manner, he could not even
give the sign post, the directing line of enunciation
which any complex novel must use at times. The
solution was Marlow, a character whose view is not
more authoritative, more of an "Idea" or a "Fact"[2]
than the rest of the book, yet whose comment steadies
the work in illumination of "the truth, manifold and
one, underlying its every aspect".

Such a method makes not only for the "sincerity"
and "truth to facts" which Conrad so prized; it also

---

[1] Crankshaw, *loc. cit.*
[2] "The thinker plunges into ideas, the scientist into facts....
It is otherwise with the artist." (*The Nigger of the Narcissus*,
Author's Preface, p. vii.)

makes for permanence. Stated in this way, the truth manifold and one is free from the colouring of temporary fashion. "He steered with care". Such a statement cannot become blunted, dated, or obsolete, as an emotional phrase might do; for instance Hardy's words about the President of the Immortals having finished his sport with Tess. By boiling the complex down to the simple, by this reduction of the one to the other, Conrad ensured its permanence.

In *Lord Jim*, as has been said, Marlow presides over what was to be the major theme of Conrad's work:

Those who read me know my conviction that the world, the temporal world, rests on a few very simple ideas: so simple that they must be as old as the hills. It rests notably, among others, on the idea of Fidelity.

(*A Personal Record*: "Familiar Preface", p. xxi)

Jim has been publicly branded as untrustworthy: the story tells of his sufferings, his attempts to regain some equally public attestation of his faithfulness.

Fidelity is for Conrad the virtue of virtues: and betrayal the crime of crimes. He had already dealt with betrayal in *Karain, The Lagoon* and the unfinished *Rescue*, and the subject fills the novels of his second period, the treatment growing more searching all the time. In *Lord Jim*, fidelity is considered as a constituent of personal honour, as it is expounded by the French lieutenant:

"I contend that one may get on knowing very well that one's courage does not come of itself (*ne vient pas*

tout seul)....But the honour—the honour, monsieur!...
The honour...that is real, that is! And what life may
be worth when"...he got on his feet with a ponderous
impetuosity as a startled ox might scramble up from
the grass..."when the honour is gone—*ah, ca! par
exemple*—I can offer no opinion. I can offer no opinion—
because—monsieur—I know nothing of it."

(*Lord Jim*, p. 148)

Personal honour, in a sense Polish and perhaps also
Latin, dominates *Lord Jim*, *The Rescue* and many
short stories. By losing his honour Jim has, for
Conrad, put himself as completely outside the pale
as Leggatt, in *The Secret Sharer*—a story written ten
years later—who committed murder, and who is his
twin. In each case a boy by a moment's blind action
is utterly ruined. It is Marlow who insists on the
irony, the incongruity between Jim and his Fate.

This was my first view of Jim. He looked as uncon-
cerned and unapproachable as only the young can look.
There he stood, clean-limbed, clean-faced, firm on his
feet, as promising a boy as ever the sun shone on, and...
I was angry as though I had detected him trying to get
something out of me by false pretences. He had no
business to look so sound.   (*Lord Jim*, p. 40)

He is

that good, stupid kind we like to feel marching right
and left of us in life....I tell you I ought to know the
right kind of looks! I would have trusted the deck to
that youngster on the strength of a single glance, and

gone to sleep with both eyes—and by Jove it wouldn't
have been safe! There are depths of horror in the
thought.   (pp. 44–5)

Here is the ironic crux. Marlow penetrates Jim's
"Don't-care-a-hang" air, through the dreadful
moment when the boy takes a chance observation
about a dog, "Look at that miserable cur", to refer
to himself, the moment when he refuses to escape
trial ("I may jump, but I don't run away"), to his
last act of immolation to the point of honour; but
this is all an unfolding of the first horrible dilemma—
the handsome, sound, sensitive boy who is ruined for
life at twenty-three. Jim cannot be reinstated in his
own eyes. It is a conception of honour which is hardly
current here; perhaps because we are not so familiar
with the state of public tyranny and corruption which
leaves a man nothing else to rely upon.

In spite of Marlow, Jim not only looks sound, but
he is sound, as even Marlow comes to recognise before
long. The momentary slip was a hideous accident,
a stroke of Fate. In this way, the tragedy of Jim does
not cut so deep as that of the later novels, for Jim is
never utterly ruined after all, since he retains both
his power of judgment and his remorse.

Lord Jim began life as a short story and grew into
a tale: *The Secret Sharer* is the perfected version,
cooler, terser, yet with far more of pity and terror.
Leggatt, who swims alongside the narrator's first
command in the dead of night, is kept secretly in the

captain's cabin for a whole voyage and dropped overboard amongst the islands of the Gulf of Siam, is, in his self-possession and despair, a slightly older Jim: "A fugitive and a vagabond on the earth, with no brand of the curse on his sane forehead to stay a slaying hand." But the strong though frustrated relationship between the Secret Sharer and the captain knits the story together more powerfully; and, though the scene of *Lord Jim* is impressive it has not the portentous horror of the island heights under which the ship is stood in dangerously close to give the murderer a chance of escape.

The black southern hill of Koh-ring seemed to hang right over the ship like a towering fragment of the everlasting night.... Then stillness again with the great shadow gliding closer, towering higher, without light, without sound. Such a hush had fallen on the ship that she might have been a bark of the dead floating in slowly under the very gate of Erebus.
"My God! where are we?"
It was the mate moaning at my elbow. (pp. 139–40)

The ship's crew see only a reckless manœuvre of their mad captain; the captain sees only a dreadful risk to his first command: but the reader feels the threat of all the material world armed against poor Leggatt, poor humanity. Conrad explicitly rejects the supernatural.[1] What he feared was the risk of personal

---

[1] "To capture the reader's attention by securing his interest and enlisting his sympathies within the limits of the visible

collapse before a hostile world. " I wondered how far I should turn out faithful to that ideal conception of one's own personality every man sets up for himself secretly ",[1] meditates the captain, and the appearance of Leggatt, his double, is the answer. In another short story which was written just after *Lord Jim, The End of the Tether*, Conrad loads the dice as heavily as possible against Captain Whalley; but the old man, simple, heroic in his integrity, is ruined only in a material sense, and when the criminal Massy tampers with the compass and wrecks the ship, Captain Whalley, in the sea tradition, can go down upon the bridge.

There remains from this early period the story which is its masterpiece, *The Heart of Darkness*. This again is taken straight from life, even such minor things as the death of the steersman being authentic. Conrad, comparing it with *Youth*, which appeared in the same volume, said:

There it was no longer a matter of sincere colouring. It was like another art altogether. That sombre theme

world and within the boundaries of human emotions." (*Typhoon, and other Stories*, Author's Note, p. vii.) "The world of the living contains enough marvels and mysteries as it is...it would almost justify the conception of life as an enchanted state. No, I am too firm in my consciousness of the marvellous to be ever fascinated by the supernatural which (take it any way you like) is but a manufactured article." (*The Shadow Line*, Author's Note, p. ix.)

[1] *The Secret Sharer* in *Twixt Land and Sea*, p. 94.

had to be given a sinister resonance, a tonality of its
own, a continued vibration that, I hoped, would hang
in the air and dwell on the ear after the last note had
been struck.   (*Youth, a Narrative and Two Other
Stories*: Author's Note, p. xi)

In this sinister resonance *The Heart of Darkness* is
supreme; and it is maintained almost wholly in terms
of the scene. It opens in the dusky Thames estuary
where Marlow is thinking "And this also has been
one of the dark places of the earth" (p. 48)—in the
days when the Romans landed. Then come his
reminiscences of the Congo trip, of the tropical
brilliance of sunshine surrounding the dying and
exploited Negroes, the dying and utterly perverted
Kurtz, equally exploited in his way, now the god of
a savage tribe, and enslaved by the primitive and
abominable lusts that burgeon from his mind in the
fecund jungle mud.

I had turned to the wilderness really, not to Mr Kurtz,
who, I was ready to admit, was as good as buried. And
for a moment it seemed to me as if I also were buried
in a vast grave full of unspeakable secrets. I felt an
intolerable weight oppressing my breast, the smell of the
damp earth, the unseen presence of victorious corruption,
the darkness of an impenetrable night.... (p. 138)

Finally after Kurtz is dead, the dying fall of
Marlow's visit to Kurtz's fiancée:

The dusk was falling. I had to wait in a lofty drawing
room, with three long windows from floor to ceiling that

were like three luminous and bedraped columns. The
bent gilt legs and backs of the furniture shone in indis-
tinct curves. The tall marble fireplace had a cold and
monumental whiteness. A grand piano stood massively
in a corner; with dark gleams on the flat surfaces like a
sombre and polished sarcophagus. A high door opened
—closed. I rose. (p. 156)

The atmosphere of the grave was not stronger in the
jungle itself. And here is the girl.

All the sad light of the cloudy evening had taken refuge
on her forehead. The fair hair, the pale visage, the
pure brow seemed surrounded by an ashy halo from
which the dark eyes looked out at me. (p. 157)

This removed, spiritual creature cherishes an
angelic illusion of the beauty of Kurtz's character,
which brings back to Marlow all the more vividly the
end of that lost soul: and, acutely haunted by Kurtz's
last words "The horror! The horror!" so that they
seem to ring in the twilit rooms, he lies the hero into
a beautiful ending.

I could not tell her. It would have been too dark—
too dark altogether. (p. 162)

And then the whole episode is at once distanced and
commented upon by the closing paragraph—a look
downstream on the darkling Thames. It is a resolu-
tion of the tragic theme which is at once simpler and
more subtle than that involving the simplest human
feelings: an effect akin to the line in Webster's
Duchess of Malfi, "Look you, the stars shine still",

or that which introduces the death scene of Shakespeare's Antony: "Sometimes we see a cloud that's
dragonish."

"We have lost the first of the ebb", said the Director
suddenly. I raised my head. The offing was barred by
a black bank of clouds, and the tranquil waterway
leading to the uttermost ends of the earth flowed sombre
under an overcast sky—seemed to lead into the heart
of an immense darkness.   (p. 162)

The story carries this particular method of suggestion to its limits. It is most delicately counter-
poised between what is seen and what is sensed or
perceived, by means of similes which transform
Conrad's powers of description into powers of analysis
and creation. With no departure from the descriptive
method, every incident yet deepens the force of the
truth manifold and one which pervades the tale.
There are contrasts and echoes: Marlow's aunt, for
instance, in her illusion that he will be an apostle of
progress in Darkest Africa provokes ironic reflections
from her nephew on the feminine powers of self-
deception, which would be wrong at the poignant
interview with the fiancée of Kurtz, but which rever-
berate there with a "sinister resonance". Again the
queer knitting women who inhabit the office in
Belgium from which this chain of exploitation starts
reoccur to Marlow at one of his worst moments as
queer things to be at the other end of this affair—and
they become shadowy Fates or at least *tricoteuses* in
recollection. The complexity is a living complexity;

and Conrad's renunciation of the supernatural gives it all the close texture of actual life. There are no occult powers among the natives, Kurtz's adorers, who are just spied at their savage rites; in the day, they are pitiful creatures frightened off by the screech of the steamer's whistle. They are even more pitiful than the starved and dying negroes of the coast or the ship's crew who are paid with brass wire but given no food, so that when the steersman is killed Marlow has to throw him overboard at once before his carcase rouses the appetite of his fellows. Yet all these figures only deepen in garish splendour the death of Kurtz— the trappings of corruption. By comparison with Kurtz, Falk, who ate human flesh himself, drew a lucky lot.

This seems the place to consider Conrad as a writer of short stories, for all his best short stories belong to his early days as a writer. In this first period he produced three volumes of tales, balanced by three in the second period. They are of very unequal interest. Conrad himself spoke slightingly of several of *Tales of Unrest* (1897), and with one exception his finest stories are in the *Youth* (1902) and *Typhoon* (1903) volumes. The exception is *The Secret Sharer*— written in November 1909, though it did not appear in book form till three years later.[1]

[1] The only volume published later than 1915 is the posthumous *Tales of Hearsay*, a miscellaneous group, of which the best, *Prince Roman*, was meant for a second book of reminiscences.

In the first rank of his tales stand *Youth, The Heart of Darkness, Falk* and *The Secret Sharer.* In the second, *The End of the Tether, A Smile of Fortune, Freya of the Seven Isles, Amy Foster* and *Typhoon.* The rest of his tales are a long way below these.

Roughly, the difference between the first group and the second is that the first are in the nature of "visions", the second are only yarns. It is not a definition or even an explanation of the short story to say that it should rise and fall in a single curve like an unbroken wave; but that is certainly true of Conrad's best stories. They present a consciousness and an event, but the colouring, the characteristic quality of the one is absolutely inseparable from the other, and all is of a piece throughout. Thus, there is greater variety of scene in *The Heart of Darkness* than in *A Smile of Fortune,* but in the one the old women in Belgium and the savages on the Congo belong to the same world, and have the same sinister colouring: whereas the resentful, savage and pathetic Alice Jacobus of *A Smile of Fortune* does not belong to the same world as the story of the deal in potatoes between the captain and her papa.

In *The Heart of Darkness* and *The Secret Sharer* the vision is of Death: the "victorious corruption" of the grave in the one, the stealthy fears of murder and retribution in the other. In *Youth* and *Falk* the vision is of Life, of simple animal vitality. *Youth* celebrates

the headlong pleasure of life, the excitement, the
readiness to take anything and to find it an adventure
which hardly survives five-and-twenty. When the
Judea's cargo blows up, carrying away the main
deck, the reaction of the young Marlow had been
"Now this is something like. This is great. I wonder
what will happen" (p. 26). "O youth!" sighs the
old Marlow.

In *Falk*, the physical vigour of Falk and his
Olympian young woman are the centre. Christian
Falk, the imperious and ruthless owner of "the only
tug on the river", is described as a "Centaur", a
man-boat. His great torso, his "immense curled
wavy beard" are known to all the river, but there
was nothing below the waist but the white lines of
the bridge screens and the churning paddles of his
tug. (Conrad disliked Freud.) Hermann's niece is
magnificently comely: "I don't mean to say she was
statuesque. She was too generously alive: but she
could have stood for an allegoric statue of the
Earth" (p. 152). The silent courtship of these two,
the primitive jealousy of Falk, the splendid description of how in sheer rage he ripped Hermann's ship
out of her berth and towed her off to sea—all con-
tribute to the central vision. "We are in his case
allowed to contemplate the foundations of all the
emotions—that one joy which is to live, and the one
sadness at the root of the innumerable torments"
(p. 224). So that even when the secret comes out,

BJC   3 and the magnificent centaur is shown as crippled by his dreadful memories of the derelict ship where he had fought for life by murder and lastly maintained it by cannibalism, even then the horrible story illustrates the same primitive vitality. "He was as frank as a child, too. He was hungry for that girl, terribly hungry, as he had been terribly hungry for food" (p. 224).

This animal vigour radiates through the story and affects not only the main characters but also the narrator, who is lively and dexterous in his manipulation of Falk and of Hermann: the Hermann family and their "patriarchal old tub"—the most clearly drawn of all Conrad's ships: and even Schomberg, who forced himself back to life again after twelve years as the villain of the novel *Victory*.

In *Youth*, the excitement of the voyage itself is more straightforwardly given. There is perfect accord between the indomitable old barque (*Judea*, London: *Do or Die*)[1] and her daredevil second mate, but in the strict sense there is no plot at all. The story foams along like a fresh sea. It is told in an easy conversational style—there are perhaps two or three passages

[1] The *Judea's* real name was the *Palestine*. There was another *Palestine* of this date, a highly respectable steamship trading between Liverpool and Boston, U.S.A., who, in the year her namesake went down, was responsible for a fine rescue operation in the Atlantic.

only of rhetorical richness and one or two of comment: but for the most part Marlow's reflections are
limited to "O youth!...Pass the bottle". The most
surprising, yet the most inevitable of the comments
comes when Marlow suddenly sees the fire which is
devouring the old ship as the same fire that burnt in
the young mate:

> I thought it fine: and the fidelity to the old ship was
> fine. We should see the last of her. O the glamour of
> youth! O the fire of it, more dazzling than the flames of
> the burning ship, throwing a magic light on the wide
> earth, leaping audaciously to the sky, presently to be
> quenched by time, more cruel, more pitiless, more bitter
> than the sea—and like the flames of the burning ship
> surrounded by an impenetrable night.   (p. 30)

The death of the old ship and the birth of Marlow
as a commander coincide. He is put in charge of the
smallest of the three boats (quite needlessly, they
could all have gone in the longboat; but they must
save as much as possible for the underwriters). Yet
these concurrent events do not sound as if they were
thought out. Indeed they are not noticed in ordinary
reading. The tale is shaped by the integrity and
spontaneity of a strong and simple feeling. It is
apparently, with *The Heart of Darkness*, the most
directly autobiographical of all Conrad's tales, and
the most quickly composed, for he wrote it all in a
few days. Though less finely wrought than *The Nigger
of the Narcissus*, it is perhaps more appealing—not

as the celebration of seamanship and its virtues, but as the lively image of a yet living past.[1]

*　　　*　　　*　　　*

The greater success of these early short stories may be explained by the comparative simplicity of interests in the early Conrad. In his later periods, he was concerned with more complex themes, more complex situations and more complex characters. Although his capacity for boiling the complex down to the simple was the special mark of his genius, this applies to the presentation and not the scope of the work. Conrad could never have seen the World in a grain of sand and Eternity in an hour, like Blake (though he might have seen it in a storm). The scope of his work became steadily wider. He introduced more characters, for instance—there are perhaps ten who count in *Lord Jim*, about thirty in *Nostromo*. The subtle and repressed characters of the later novels require some room to unfold themselves, and *The Secret Sharer* succeeds so consummately only because in that case there can be no development— the bounds are reached at the beginning. Besides, the story has links with the novels—notably, as has been said, with *Lord Jim*—and the theme came to Conrad's hands softened and plastic with handling. It provides the perfect psychological case—the

[1] Conrad actually seems to have been an irresponsible youth, maturing late, not thinking of his career and causing much anxiety to his excellent uncle Tadeusz.

hidden self "exactly the same" as the other, but guilty, and always of necessity concealed from the eyes of the world; dressed in a sleeping suit, the garb of the unconscious life, appearing and disappearing out of, and into, the infinite sea.

In the short stories of the second period, the moods and stories of the novels of that period appear in cruder, more intensified, more fantastic forms. There is *Gaspar Ruiz*, a sort of pendant to *Nostromo*; the heavy, flabby Mr Jacobus of *A Smile of Fortune* with his thick lips glued together and his sleepy self-assurance—a miniature of Mr Verloc, the hero of *The Secret Agent*. Conrad even repeats himself from story to story: *The Partner* is simply *The End of the Tether* in a different setting, and *Typhoon* is modelled on *Youth*, and *The Nigger*.

Conrad seems to have approached his short stories in two ways: either as deliberate exercises in technique, or as neurotic safety valves. Thus practically all the stories in *A Set of Six* are the equivalent of a pianist's "scales", useful, inevitable—but not music. Conrad is too clearly out to improve his technique: sometimes merely to be tidy.[1] When he says

---

[1] "In that collection I aimed at a certain virtuosity of style" (*Life and Letters*, vol. II, p. 66). "Take the volume of *Youth* which in its component parts presents the three ages of man (for that is what it really is, and I knew very well what I was about when I wrote *The End of the Tether* to be the last of that trio)" (*ibid.* p. 338).

For if there is to be any classification by subjects,
I have done two Storm-pieces in *The Nigger of the
Narcissus* and *Typhoon*; and two Calm-pieces, this one
[*The Secret Sharer*] and *The Shadow Line*.

(*Twixt Land and Sea*, Author's Note, p. ix)

it recalls the pairs of prints (Highland Cattle and
The Monarch of The Glen) which in unfailing sym-
metry decorated the drawing rooms of the 'eighties.
On the other hand, Conrad would let himself go in
the short story, and dramatise his own misery and
fears under the figure of the Polish castaway in *Amy
Foster*; or give vent to the terror of madness and
disorder which lies behind his insistence on law and
discipline, in *Freya of the Seven Isles*. All the stories
in the two volumes *Twixt Land and Sea* (1912) and
Within the Tides (1915) are not only painful but they
depict helpless, fixed, unmitigated suffering, and in
most cases an actively malignant character who is
responsible for the suffering, robbing it of the dignity
and inherent justification that attend on natural
calamity. In the short stories, the reader is nearest
to Conrad the man, the writer of so many agonised
letters—"One goes through with it—and there's
nothing to show at the end. Nothing! Nothing!
Nothing!" (*Life and Letters*, vol. I, p. 283). "Not
extinction. Not yet. All of you stand by me so nobly
that I must still exist" (*ibid.* p. 299). It is this sheer
pain which appears when Heemskirk deliberately
strands Jasper's pretty brig upon the sand, and leaves

Jasper to degradation, poverty and madness, and Freya to die of a broken heart. Conrad was always pessimistic about the facts of the world, but generally he was not overwhelmed by them.

The romantic feeling of reality was in me an inborn faculty. This in itself may be a curse, but when disciplined by a sense of personal responsibility and a recognition of the hard facts of existence shared with the rest of mankind becomes but a point of view from which the very shadows of life appear endowed with an internal glow. And such romanticism is not a sin. It is none the worse for the knowledge of truth. It only tries to make the best of it, hard as it may be; and in this hardness discovers a certain aspect of beauty.

(*Within the Tides*, Author's Note, pp. vii–viii)[1]

Though he looked on any attempt to interpret the universe as friendly to man in the light of a "great Joke", Conrad's "hard facts of existence" included spiritual facts. The virtue of the novels lies precisely in that the vision of evil is so strong as to be very nearly omnipotent—but not quite. They show that ability to face the worst that the writer can frankly conceive—not to deal with it, just to face it—which is the distinctive quality of tragedy. In some of the

[1] The dedication of *Within the Tides* as "this sheaf of care-free ante-bellum pages" is one of the few cases when Conrad provides an unconscious joke. The centre of every one of these stories is a violent death—murder or suicide or both. And they are not easy deaths either!

tales, however, there is something worse than facing of the evil vision; there is an obsession by it. The later stories are perhaps best regarded as necessary by-products of the great period; gold dust from that mine. There are finds to be made among them: but in general the interest is on bigger things.

II. THE HOLLOW MEN

THE change which came over Conrad's work with *Nostromo* was not surprising. He was now established as an author, and his sailor's life had receded:[1] his fits of despair and the difficulty in composition were increasing: the influence of Flaubert was replaced by that of Henry James, upon whom Conrad wrote a study at this time. These circumstances may be reflected in the deepening power of his subjects, which become more tragic and more introverted, and also in the correspondingly deeper powers of technique.

All the great figures of this period of his work—Gian' Battista and Monygham in *Nostromo*, Razumov, Renouard, Flora, Heyst,[2] have in common with Lord Jim a profound self-distrust. They have lost their trust in themselves, but they have not lost their beliefs, and so they are tormented by their failure, or what they think their failure, to live up to those principles in which they most deeply believe. The temptations differ: Gian' Battista the Incorruptible is tempted by the lighter full of silver and steals it:

[1] Of the two long stories with a sea setting written after this date, *The Rescue* had been begun as early as 1897, and *Chance* was started in 1906.

[2] Also Arlette and Eugène Réal in *The Rover*, who have been numbed and frozen by childhood spent in the horrors of the French Revolution.

Dr Monygham has been tortured into denouncing his
friends for imaginary crimes and can never recover
his self-respect, or forgive Nostromo the ostentation
of his integrity; Razumov also betrays his friends:
Flora—a complete case of the inferiority complex
conceived before that term was invented—feels a
burden upon all her friends through "the scar of the
blow received in childhood"; Heyst is a sceptical
pessimist and stoic, and most fully enunciates the
philosophy of the group. To be passionately concerned for your principles, yet to conceive depths on
depths of self-betrayal: that is the crux. *The Secret
Agent* depicts more passive and more helpless sufferers;
in this book it is the senseless cruelty of blind lives
that Conrad is contemplating, and the betrayal of a
blind love.

Such are the dominant themes of the period, which
seem to spring from Conrad's Polish heritage. As his
sea life receded, his childhood revived—Siberia, a
mother virtually murdered by the brutalities imposed on her when she shared his father's exile—
uncles, cousins killed or broken, wrecked homes and
secret conspiracies. Suffering of a width and intensity
then unknown in Western Europe put terrific pressure
behind his pen, and there was personal suffering too,
for his melancholia was at times so intense that his
letters make altogether intolerable reading.[1] He was

[1] The short stories of this period, particularly *Amy Foster,
Freya of the Seven Isles, A Smile of Fortune* and *The Planter
of Malata*, are more unremittedly painful than the novels.

poor, and often ill, but his black fits would give to any external misfortune the comforting feeling of a counter irritant.

Yet to many critics the novels of this period present themselves mainly as experiments in technique. Mr Edward Crankshaw's penetrating study[1] would almost make of Conrad another Henry James. It is true that the construction changes and becomes more complex. Except in *Chance*, which hung over from 1906 to 1911, Marlow does not reappear; and even there Marlow is helped by a series of reporters which greatly complicates matters.

Conrad developed a new type of construction involving the use of a time-shift, and of a consistent irony. In the earlier works, irony was rare, and the parts of the tales had reinforced the whole by an intensification of the detail, by the power of implication. Now, the different parts are played off, telescoped together, interwoven or run into each other. There are several stories in *Nostromo*, but all illustrate the corrupting power of the silver mine, of the "material interests";[2] the ruin of Gian' Battista, the

[1] See p. 21, note 1.

[2] See *Life and Letters*, vol. II, p. 296: "I will take the liberty to point out that Nostromo has never been intended for the hero of the Tale of the Seaboard. Silver is the pivot of moral and material events, affecting the lives of everybody in the tale.... The word *silver* occurs almost at the very beginning of the story proper and I took care to introduce it into the very last paragraph, which perhaps would have been better without the phrase which contains that key word."

damning success of Don Carlos Gould, the spiritual
defeat of Mrs Gould, the death of Don José, the
suicide of Decoud. In *Lord Jim* there had been only
one story. Melodic variations on a theme are replaced
by harmonic variations.

Nostromo cost Conrad more to write than any of
his books: the well-known account in *A Personal
Record* describes the anguish of this "stérilité d'un
écrivain nerveux":

For twenty months, neglecting the common joys of
life that fall to the lot of the humblest on this earth, I had
like the prophet of old "wrestled with the Lord" for my
creation.... These are perhaps strong words, but it is
difficult to characterise otherwise the intimacy and the
strain of a creative effort in which mind and will and
conscience are engaged to the full, hour after hour, day
after day, away from the world and to the exclusion of
all that makes life really lovable and gentle—something
for which a material parallel can only be found in the
everlasting sombre stress of the westward winter passage
round Cape Horn.... I suppose I went to bed sometimes and got up the same number of times. Yes,
I suppose I slept, and ate the food put before me,
and talked connectedly to my household on suitable
occasions. But I had never been aware of the even
flow of daily life, made easy and noiseless for me by
a silent, watchful, tireless affection. Indeed, it seemed
to me that I had been sitting at that table surrounded
by the litter of a desperate fray for days and nights
on end.

(*A Personal Record*, pp. 98–100)

Nostromo was not a public success, at least not a financial success. The public who had thought the men of the *Narcissus* "engaging ruffians" because they used strong language were not likely to understand the subtle counterpoint of this book. For each character illustrates the play of material interests, and all are set in a country which is completely realised—its "history, geography, politics, finance" and all its detail from "the unresting batteries of stamps" clattering out the ingots at San Tomé to the hens in the yard of the Italian *albergo* "making off in all directions with immense strides" before the impassioned, profound, vibrating tones of the black-browed Signora Teresa. The scene of *Nostromo* is indeed its most impressive effect. The whole civilisation of nineteenth-century Latin America is presented: implicitly in the figure of Antonia there is also present the emotional reverberations from Conrad's Polish youth.[1] The sweep of the survey is widened by Conrad's use of a broken time-sequence. He works backwards and forwards round the revolution and counter-revolution which are the centre of the book, covering directly perhaps fifteen or twenty years.

The characters are very subtly balanced. Two men of the people—Georgio Viola the idealistic Garibaldino, and Nostromo, the "Incorruptible", the simple egoistic natural leader—are set against the

---

[1] This is acknowledged in the "Author's Note".

ex-ambassador Don José, who shares the integrity of
Viola, and Charles Gould, the Administrator of the
Mine, who pins his faith to material interests. "'They
are bound to impose the conditions in which alone
they can continue to exist. That's how your money-
making is justified here in the face of lawlessness and
disorder. It is justified because the security which it
demands must be shared with an oppressed people'"
(*Nostromo*, p. 84). Nostromo is corrupted and brought
low by the silver of the mine: the new state which
Don José dies in creating becomes subservient to the
great material interests: Charles Gould grows enslaved by the forces he has created, and judgment is
pronounced on him by Dr Monygham, the only man
of integrity left at the end; Dr Monygham, who
had been broken by torture, and who had said even
to his idol, Mrs Gould, "'Really, it is most unreason-
able to demand that a man should think of other
people so much better than he is able to think of
himself'" (*Nostromo*, pp. 44–5).[1] The new state is an
advance on the old, as described by the cynical
Decoud:

> Imagine an atmosphere of the opéra bouffe, in which
> all the comic business of stage statesmen, brigands etc.
> etc. all their farcical stealing, intriguing, stabbing, is done
> in dead earnest. It is screamingly funny....
>
> (*Nostromo*, p. 152)

[1] Renouard, in *The Planter of Malata*, and Razumov, in
Under Western Eyes, seem to be developments or variations

But Nostromo is left miserably dying, Mrs Gould "as completely alone as any human being on this earth" and the two old men are dead. Dr Monygham echoes unconsciously the speech of Charles Gould:

There is no peace and no rest in the development of material interests. They have their law and their justice. But it is founded on expediency, and is inhuman; it is without rectitude, without the continuity and the force that can be found only in a moral principle. Mrs Gould, the time approaches when all the Gould Concession stands for shall weigh as heavily upon the people as the barbarism, cruelty and misrule of a few years back.

(*Nostromo*, p. 511)[1]

Yet the end is not unresolved tragedy. Out in the great Golfo Placido beyond the harbour, the gulf whose calms had protected Sulaco from civilisation and its miseries in earlier days, the family of Viola keep a lighthouse, which stands upon the very island concealing Nostromo's treasure of stolen silver. As Viola's eldest daughter, standing on the balcony of the lighthouse, hears the news of Nostromo's death shouted up by Dr Monygham, she cries his name

upon Dr Monygham: Renouard in his hopeless passion for Felicia Moorsom, and Razumov in his betrayal and remorse.
[1] The exploitation of the people by material interests disguised as progress is of course part of the theme of *The Heart of Darkness*, but there it is much less of a "problem" to be considered, owing to the difference in intention and in the scale of the story.

aloud in anguish, and so, in the last words of the
book,

the genius of the magnificent Capitaz de Cargadores
dominated the dark gulf containing his conquests of
treasure and love.   (*Nostromo*, p. 566)

*   *   *   *

In contrast with the richness of *Nostromo*, there is
in *The Secret Agent* practically no other scene than
that of Mr Verloc's shop of shady wares, no other
characters than the Verloc family. The story has for
its main event a "senseless outrage" staged by Verloc
the *agent provocateur*, which unexpectedly involves
the death of his feeble-minded young brother-in-law.
Mrs Verloc, whose maternal passion for Stevie is the
mainspring of her simple existence, and who has never
suspected her husband's activities, kills Verloc, and
then in blind terror puts herself into the hands of one
of the revolutionary party, who leaves her stranded
on the Calais steamer. She throws herself overboard
in despair.

Such is the story, but its melodramatic events are
all told with a deliberate and consistent foreshortening.
They are described purely externally, and always
with an ironic overtone. The external point of view
exactly fits the limited intellects of the actors—
Verloc is sluggishly stupid, Mrs Verloc is obstinately
governed by her *idée fixe*, which is Stevie's welfare,
the revolutionaries are fanatics or brutes—but the

ironic overtone represents Conrad's own "pity and scorn" at the frustration of these lives. The account of the Verloc *ménage*, at the moment when the disclosure is made, will show the mixture of simplicity and irony:

Mrs Verloc pursued the visions of seven years' security for Stevie, loyally paid for on her part: of security growing into confidence, into a domestic feeling, stagnant and deep like a placid pool.... The silence in the kitchen was prolonged, and Mr Verloc felt disappointed. He had expected his wife to say something.... Yet the occasion did not, he recognised, demand speech from her.... Their accord was perfect but it was not precise. It was a tacit accord, congenial to Mrs Verloc's incuriosity and to Mr Verloc's habits of mind, which were indolent and secret. They refrained from going to the bottom of facts and motives.... *(The Secret Agent*, pp. 243–5)

So the scene goes on in the stuffy cosiness of the lighted kitchen behind the shop, with a faithful account of the surface thoughts of these two, who are so inarticulate that their surface thoughts are little more than records of sensation and instinct, till

He saw partly on the ceiling and partly on the wall the moving shadow of an arm with a clenched hand holding a carving knife. It flickered up and down. Its movements were leisurely enough for Mr Verloc to recognise the limb and the weapon....

They were leisurely enough for Mr Verloc to elaborate a plan of defence involving a dash behind the table, and the felling of the woman to the ground with a heavy

wooden chair. But they were not leisurely enough to
allow Mr Verloc time to move either hand or foot....
Mr Verloc, the Secret Agent, turning slightly on his side
with the force of the blow, expired without stirring a
limb, in the muttered sound of the word "Don't" by
way of protest.   (*The Secret Agent*, pp. 262–3)

The consistency of the writing does not preclude
contrast. As Mr Crankshaw says, the whole affair is
isolated and cut off from the run of normal existence,
and placed under a glass bell which, according to the
incidence of the angle of the light, has a more or less
distorting effect on the objects. But provided he does
not break the glass, Conrad can vary the light in-
definitely. As Henry James would remark, it is
"supremely difficult". It differs radically from the
work of Henry James himself in being so concrete.
The colours, sounds, smells of the Verloc home are
almost suffocatingly present to the reader; whereas
in James's world of mental relationships, hints, currents of feeling, the external world of sense hardly
ever directly intrudes.[1] Hence when James praised
Chance for its tackling of the most difficult subject in
the most difficult way, this seems also a transference
from his own habits.[2] But yet, in contrast with the
sordid welter under the glass bell of *The Secret Agent*,
it is true to say that *Chance* is complicated by its

[1] E.g. there is the celebrated refusal to explain the nature of
the source of the Newcome wealth in *The Ambassadors*.

[2] Henry James, *Notes on Novelists* (J. M. Dent, 1914,
p. 274).

whole series of narrations within narrations, like wheels within wheels, and also by its dislocated time-sequence, working backwards and forwards in the manner of *Nostromo*. The use of Marlow and the other narrators in *Chance* "represents" for James "the protagonist in face of the powers leagued against it ".[1] It is the tortuous involutions of Flora's mind which are the justification not only of Marlow but of all the minor characters, "the Powells, the Franklins, the Fynes, the tell-tale little dogs".[1] But throughout *Chance* the writing is far too rich, the colouring too strong for any of the characters to be looked on as mere means for extracting more from the "main dear delicate situation", like Maria Gostry in *The Ambassadors* or Van in *The Awkward Age*. They exist in their own right, down to the tell-tale little dog:

The dog became at once wildly demonstrative, half strangling himself in his collar, his eyes and tongue hanging out in the excess of his incomprehensible affection for me. This was before he caught sight of the cake in my hand. A series of vertical springs high up in the air followed, and then, when he got the cake, he instantly lost his interest in everything else. (p. 142)

And so on, for half a page, on the way the Fynes treated their dog (of course he was brought up hygienically and ought not to have been given any cake).

[1] Henry James, *Notes on Novelists* (J. M. Dent, 1914, pp. 277, 278).

In fact the main impression, especially compared
with *The Secret Agent* and *Under Western Eyes*, is of
a rich, full vitality. Flora, beaten by the shock of
her abominable governess's cruelty, and her father's
imprisonment, the long sordid stretches of her life
while he was in jail, and her last final betrayal by
Captain Antony himself, who thinking she has turned
to him out of sheer despair, decides that their marriage ought to be only nominal—Flora is in the long
line of Conrad's frustrated heroines, and the sister to
Natalie Haldin of *Under Western Eyes*,[1] even as
Marlow here in his rehabilitated form replaces the
"teacher of languages" who is Natalie's confidant
and tells her tale.[2] But whereas in *Under Western
Eyes* the unremitting pressure of misery and crime

[1] Natalie's brother was sentenced to death for assassination,
and her love for Razumov only deepened her misery, for it
drove him to confess that he had betrayed her brother.
"She raised her grey eyes slowly. Shadows seemed to come
and go in them, as if the steady flame of her soul had been
made to vacillate at last in the cross currents of poisoned air
from the corrupted dark immensity claiming her for its own,
where virtues themselves fester into crimes in the cynicism of
oppression and revolt. 'It is impossible to be more un-
happy....' The languid whisper of her voice struck me with
dismay. 'It is impossible. I feel my heart becoming like
ice'" (p. 356).
[2] In *Under Western Eyes* there are several sources of information: the diary of Razumov, the old teacher's story,
and the stories of the revolutionaries. In *Chance* there are
also several sources: Marlow, Powell, and the Fynes.

chokes every vital impulse and leaves only an ex-
hausted calm at the end of the book, in *Chance* the
triumphant ending only confirms Antony and Powell
in an ascendance that was theirs from the beginning.

Conrad lets himself go on Roderick Antony. He is
a sailor; he tramps the poop, he clips his speech, he
is impetuous, generous, exacting, affectionate, unselfconscious: he is heroic to the point of absurdity:[1]
and he goes down with his ship. The unself consciousness
ness of Antony is the corollary of his power for
sweeping action; his active life leaves him like Othello
with a suppressed capacity for passion, and with
Othello's inexperience and trustfulness.[2]

Having himself always said exactly what he meant,
he imagined that people (unless they were liars, which
of course his brother-in-law could not be) never said
more than they meant.
                                        (*Chance*, p. 329)

So when his brother-in-law, Fyne, the admirable civil
servant, tells him that Flora is only marrying him
out of destitution and desperation, Antony, "intoxi-
cated with the generosity and pity of his part",

hit upon that renunciation at which one does not know

[1] "There are several kinds of heroism and one of them at
least is idiotic. It is the one which wears the aspect of sublime
delicacy" (p. 328).
[2] "With his beard cut to a point, his swarthy sunburnt
complexion, thin nose and his lean head there was something
African, something Moorish in Captain Antony" (p. 424).

whether to grin or shudder....It was a love born of
that rare pity which is not akin to contempt because
rooted in an overwhelmingly strong capacity for tenderness—the tenderness of the fiery predatory kind....At the
same time I am forced to think that his vanity must have
been enormous.

(*Chance*, p. 331)

The wretched Flora, already "bewildered in
quivering hopelessness by gratuitous cruelty: self-
confidence destroyed and instead a resigned reck-
lessness, a mournful callousness", takes this as only
another proof of her mysterious power of antagonising
people and earning their contempt. The false situation, intensified by their cramped quarters at sea—
for of course Antony's predatory tenderness will not
leave Flora ashore—would hardly persist were it not
for the intrusion of a third party—Flora's father the
ex-financier and ex-convict, the great Mr de Barral.
Reduced by his "wrongs" to an embodiment of
resentment and contempt, possessively jealous of
Flora's marriage, by a marvellous final stroke he
sees life aboard ship as an extension of his prison life,
the *Ferndale* as a floating jail. His neurotic hatred of
his confinement turning to hatred of Antony—who,
if not exactly neurotic, is repressing himself into a
state of nervous tension—creates a situation of triple
frustration which is kept up in the most masterly
way. Being a frail and dependent old man, de Barral
does not say what he means: he takes to plotting on

the sly,[1] and his cold Iago-like malignancy finally
leads him to an attempt to poison Captain Antony,
and this leads to the dénouement. For Powell, the
mate, sees him and warns Antony, who is "disarmed
before the other's mad and sinister sincerity". And
then comes the keyword of the book: "Only the
normal can overcome the abnormal." Antony col-
lapses, tells Flora she can leave him: Flora, goaded
beyond all caring, breaks the vicious circle:

Mrs Antony's voice reached Powell's ears, entreating
and indignant.

"You can't cast me off like this, Roderick. I won't go
away from you—I won't...."

Powell turned about and discovered then that what
"Mr Smith" was puckering his eyes at was the sight of
his daughter clinging round Captain Antony's neck....
Mrs Antony's hair hung back in a dark mass like the hair
of a drowned woman. She looked as if she would let go
and sink to the floor if the captain were to withhold his
sustaining arm. But the captain obviously had no such
intention.   (*Chance*, p. 430)

That however is not the end of the story. Antony
is allowed to enjoy his triumph, and then he is most
unceremoniously killed off, in order that the silent
devotion of Powell may be rewarded with the hand
of his widow. The reason is twofold: Powell belongs

---

[1] "There was a red patch on each of his old soft cheeks, as
if somebody had been pinching them. He drooped his head
and looked with a sort of underhand expectation at the
Captain and Mrs Antony" (p. 425).

to the frame of the narration, and by this last move
Mrs Antony is brought out of the picture into contact
with actuality in the second degree—that is, with
Powell and Marlow. Moreover, Powell is an even
more drastic example of the simple sailor, without
Captain Antony's poetic ancestry and "idiotic delicacy". And in this book the simplicity of sea life
is its greatest virtue; a sanative simplicity which is
certainly "looked down on"—in a wholly laudatory
sense—by Conrad and by Marlow. Antony says:

"It ought to teach you not to make rash surmises.
You should leave that to the shore people. They are
great hands at spying out something wrong. I dare say
they know what they have made of the world. A damn'
poor job they make of it, and that's plain. Its a con-
foundedly ugly place, Mr Franklin. You don't know
anything of it? Well, no—we sailors don't...."
Franklin was impressed by this unexpected lecture
upon the wickedness of the solid world surrounded by
the salt incorruptible waters on which he and his captain
had dwelt all their lives in happy innocence.

(Chance, pp. 270–1)

Powell, who has no character of his own but is just
the embodiment of seafaring, can be more penetrating
on the subject:

"The thought that I was done with the earth for
many many months to come made me feel very quiet
and self-contained as it were. Sailors will understand
what I mean."

Marlow nodded. " It is a strictly professional feeling ",
he commented....

" I should call it the peace of the sea ", said Mr Charles
Powell in an earnest tone, but looking at us as though he
half expected to be met by a laugh of derision.

(*Chance*, pp. 31–2)[1]

There is something rather dangerous in such a use
of the term " professional ". Conrad is getting nostalgic
and a bit sentimental: he has really forgotten the sea,
and he is getting too conscious about it. So the
Secret Sharer says: " A nice position for a *Conway*
boy ", about as likely a remark as that an Etonian
who had just committed murder should say, " A nice
position for an Etonian ". *The Mirror of the Sea*
summed up and ended that side of Conrad's life. It
is a beautiful book; a little too beautiful. Its unpopu-
larity distressed him, but even those who love the sea
find it a little rich, a little overcharged. So a man
might in all sincerity attempt the portrait of a dead
wife or mother; it would be too beautiful; it is
impossible not to idealise the dead. Conrad veered
between exasperation at his reputation ("Do try to
keep the damned sea out of it. My interests are
terrestrial after all ")[2] and the very conscious rôle of
the Old Salt, as played in his Admiralty articles, his
correspondence with Mr Laurence Holt, and on his

[1] Cf. also *A Smile of Fortune* in *Twixt Land and Sea*, p. 90;
and *The Secret Sharer* in *ibid.* p. 107.
[2] R. Curle, *The Last Twelve Years of Joseph Conrad*, p. 41.

voyage to America. (Of course he hated the *Majestic*: she made him feel so out of date.)

Nevertheless, there is a growing sense of confidence about *Chance*, even on occasion a touch of condescension towards his characters, that just spoils the flavour of his humour, as in the phrase " The captain obviously had no such intention ". The telescoping of the time-sequence which is needed to get the maximum pressure on the climax—the weeks of tension on board the *Ferndale* when the false situation was at its height—is done with an easy assurance which cannot be felt in the more rigid construction of *The Secret Agent* and *Under Western Eyes*. The book was Conrad's greatest material success, and made his reputation as a popular author. There can be no doubt that this was due to the romantic love story, the full and pulsing style, and perhaps to that happy air of ease which pervaded the darkest revelations of the life of de Barral and Flora. Conrad's style was certainly flowing more readily. The conversations and the rhetorical description balanced each other better than they had done before. "Idiomatically I am never at fault"[1] he once boasted, and he succeeded also in catching the exact intonation of the speech. For example, the preoccupation of Powell, going off to visit Mrs Antony, is here contrasted by means of the verbs with the determination of Marlow to sug-

---

[1] *Life and Letters*, vol. II, p. 296. Not strictly true: e.g. he never mastered "shall" and "will".

gest to the simple sailor that he ought to marry her.

"Listen, Powell", I said, "We got to know each other quite by chance?"

"Oh, quite!" he admitted, adjusting his hat.

"And the science of life consists in seizing every chance that presents itself", I pursued. "Do you believe that?"

"Gospel truth", he declared innocently.

"Well, don't forget it."   (*Chance*, p. 446)

Conrad's descriptive rhetoric is the most characteristic part of his style, and perhaps it could only have been achieved by one to whom English was not the mother tongue. The Polish student of Jeremy Taylor could combine magnificence and sincerity in a way that no native could have done without self-consciousness.[1] The famous final paragraphs of *The Heart of Darkness* and *Nostromo*—the whole of *The Mirror of the Sea*—the seascapes of *Chance* have a deliberate richness of rhythm and a lavish sensuousness which remain quite sound, untouched by any vulgar ostentation; but Conrad was enabled to do this because the language was to him a medium, in a sense in which to an Englishman it can never be a medium: and also because he set himself such a rigid standard of emotional integrity. His manifesto, the "Familiar Preface" to *A Personal Record*, declares:

There are some of us to whom an open display of sentiment is repugnant....It may be pride. There can

[1] Examples are given in the Prologue.

be nothing more humiliating than to see the shaft of
one's emotions miss the mark of either laughter or tears.
...And then—it is very difficult to be wholly joyous or
wholly sad on this earth.... The fact is, I have a positive
horror of losing even for one moving moment that full
possession of myself which is the first condition of good
service. And I have carried over my notion of good
service from my earlier into my later existence.... I have
always suspected in the effort to bring into play the
extremities of emotions the debasing touch of insincerity.
In order to move others we must deliberately allow our-
selves to be carried away beyond the bounds of our
normal sensibility...the danger lies in the writer becoming the victim of his own exaggeration.... An historian of hearts is not an historian of emotions, yet he
penetrates further, restrained as he may be, since his
aim is to touch the very fount of laughter and tears. The
sight of human affairs deserves admiration and pity.
They are worthy of respect too. And he is not insensitive
who pays them the undemonstrative tribute of a sigh
which is not a sob, and of a smile which is not a grin.

(*A Personal Record*, pp. xviii–xxi)

The passage itself has a conscious rhetoric, and even,
when Conrad speaks of his notions of good service,
an emotion which may seem to contradict the tenor
of its meaning. But it has been shown that Conrad
does limit himself in his portrayal of the emotions,
and thereby gains the power to reduce and mutate
the implied—but suppressed—feelings and to crystal-
lise them out with greater purity and permanence in
some symbolic description of an external scene or a

human form. Conrad's world is almost achingly
solid: you bump against bulkheads, your throat is
scalded with hot coffee, the wind whips your face
scarlet and makes your eyes water. Yet somehow
there is a curious feeling that all is a shell.[1] His
women, except for Flora, and perhaps—but not
certainly—Mrs Gould, are treated with such restraint
that they seem almost too aërial for this workaday
world: though no one could more delicately convey
the enchantment—a favourite word of Conrad—
"the charm of that mortal flesh". And then suddenly,
effortlessly, with an easy stroke he will achieve complete humanity—the completer for his restraint,
though it seems too universalised to make the characters who exhibit it any more clear as precise and
particular persons—they take on at such moments
a representative function. This is the last reward of
boiling the complex down to the simple. The most
moving example is that occasion when in *Victory* the
waif Lena, killed in saving her lover, appeals to him
in her last utterance of ignorance and trust.

The faint smile on her deep-cut lips waned, and her
head sank deep into the pillow, taking on the majestic

[1] It is a more than usual awareness of the world together
with a strange feeling of detachment or dissociation from it.
This feeling can be induced by drugs, but it is normal to
certain psychological types. Perhaps Conrad's "stérilités",
his dreadful difficulty in writing, may have sprung from the
feeling that everything had to be spun out of himself—
because of this dissociation, this lack of "contact".

pallor and immobility of marble. But over the muscles, which seemed set in their transfigured beauty for ever, passed a slight and awful tremor. With amazing strength she asked loudly:

"What's the matter with me?"

"You have been shot, dear Lena", Heyst said in a steady voice, whilst Davidson, at the question, turned away and leant his head against the post at the foot of the bed.

"Shot? I did think, too, that something had struck me."

(*Victory*, p. 406)

Victory is the last novel of this period, and if not the greatest, it is the most firmly modelled, the most boldly wrought. The characters are drastically simplified, and take on something of the quality of figures in a morality play; each represents a facet of experience, or a type of mind, and with statuesque impressiveness they remain fixed in that representative pose throughout the simple narrative of few, violent and sudden events. Conrad himself said: "It is a book in which I have tried to grasp at more life stuff than perhaps in any other of my works" (*Life and Letters*, vol. II, p. 342). On the only occasion when he gave a public reading from his works, he chose to read the death of Lena.

Baron Heyst, the last of the "Hollow Men", is also the most completely disillusioned. Generous, chivalrous, tender-hearted as he is, he is hopelessly crippled by his nihilistic view of life, inherited and imposed on him by his father the philosopher, of whom he says:

Suppose the world were a factory and all mankind workmen in it. Well, he discovered that the wages were not good enough. That they were paid in counterfeit money.

(*Victory*, pp. 195–6)

In his scepticism, Heyst denies not only the justice of the world but even the validity of human relationships. The earlier figures, the Goulds, Razumov and Natalie, Flora and Antony, suffered from incomplete and frustrated relationships; but Heyst entirely repudiates them. "We perish'd, each alone."

One gets attached in a way to people one has done something for. But is that friendship? I am not sure what it was. I only know that he who forms a tie is lost. The germ of corruption has entered into his soul.

(*Victory*, pp. 199–200)

The world went by appearance and called us friends, as far as I can remember. Appearance—what more, what better can you ask for? In fact, you can't have better. You can't have anything else.

(*Victory*, p. 204)

Consequently, paralysed by his stoic creed and his reflective habits—"the most pernicious of all habits found in civilised man"—Heyst strives to become the man of universal detachment, detached, like Hamlet, from even life itself.

I may truly say, too, that I never did care, I won't say for life—I had scorned what people call by that name

from the first—but for being alive. I don't know if that
is what men call courage, but I doubt it very much.

(*Victory*, p. 212)

Yet it is Heyst who carries off to his solitary island
station Lena, the poor cockney girl from Zangia-
como's Ladies' Orchestra, an outcast like Flora, but
a child of the people, unselfconscious, illiterate, and
downtrodden. He does this out of necessity, for Lena
is being persecuted by Schomberg, aided by Zangia-
como, but by the act his "heart is broken into, all
sorts of weaknesses are free to enter". Even for
Lena, he cannot conquer his "infernal mistrust of all
life".

Heyst, with his irony, his stoicism, is plainly very
close to part of Conrad himself. His irony has the
accent of Conrad: his protective humour is of the
same kind too, and has often the same uneasy air
of patronage. Heyst might have written some of
Conrad's stories—*The End of the Tether, Freya of the
Seven Isles, The Partner, Amy Foster*. But here Heyst
is projected, exorcised, as perhaps Lord Jim exorcised
an earlier Conrad.[1] Also by his relation to the other
characters, Heyst is "placed" and valued.

[1] In *The Polish Heritage of Joseph Conrad* (Sampson Low,
1930) Dr Gustaf Morf attempts an elucidation of Conrad's
novels in terms of his psychology. He classes Conrad as
belonging to Jung's "intuitive" type and sees in many of the
novels a projection of Conrad's personal conflicts. Thus he
believes Conrad was haunted by a fear of having betrayed
the patriotic traditions of his family by leaving Poland,

Against the nihilism of Heyst is set the nihilism of "Mr Jones". Mr Jones is a gentleman without a history. His appearance is spectral (Davy Jones is the sailor's name for death) and he says to Heyst "I am he who is". He has had other formulas: Milton's was "Myself am hell", and Shelley's "He who reigns". He is the Living Skeleton, the Heart of Darkness.

Mr Jones is attended by Ricardo, the ordinary criminal, and by Pedro, the ordinary savage; "A spectre, a cat, and an ape", as Schomberg sees them (p. 148). The central situation places these three upon Heyst's island, prepared to rob and if necessary kill him for a hypothetical hoard of wealth, which in fact does not exist. Heyst is slowly coming to feel in the company of Lena, with her simple common speech and her lovely voice, "a greater sense of his own reality than he had ever known in his life" (p. 200). But the arrival of the nightmarish trio although he left on the advice of his elders; and this, he thinks, is symbolised in Jim's desertion of the *Patna*, while physically Jim is a *compensatory* figure. Dr Morf sees also a projection of Conrad in the figure of Martin Decoud, and his fate symbolises what Conrad fears for himself—an end of loneliness and despair. The captains in *The Secret Sharer* and *The Shadow Line* dramatise Conrad's fears about his ability to live up to the exaggerated personal standard he set up: whilst the Polish hero of *Amy Foster* stands quite unambiguously for Conrad's hidden fears about himself, which are more indirectly expressed in *An Outpost of Progress* and *The Heart of Darkness.*

paralyses him, as the nightmarish Gentleman Brown had paralysed Lord Jim, and perhaps for the same reason—because of the common element of disbelief and scepticism which is mutual to Heyst and Mr Jones.[1] At all events, he is disarmed and at their mercy, and yet in his trapped helplessness he is responsible for the safety of Lena. But Lena, whose devotion and strength are quite unsuspected by Heyst, is perfectly prepared to sacrifice her life for him, and by deliberately enticing the amorous Ricardo, she gains possession of his weapon—at the cost of suggesting to Heyst that she is faithless and of being shot by Mr Jones. But she has saved Heyst. Unconscious alike of his suspicions and his remorse, she dies in complete and innocent triumph.

Such is the story, and its bare outline may over-stress the intellectual structure, what might be loosely called the "problem" of the book. The tale is simply told; there is no narrator's perspective, there is neither irony, humour nor comment in the telling: the irony, the humour and the comments, such as they are, belong to Heyst.[2] Yet the book is the completest vindication of the values represented by

[1] Gentleman Brown represents the profession Jim has disgraced, though he is more of a disgrace to it than Jim. Heyst has never betrayed a trust—he is scrupulously faithful to all his obligations: but he has betrayed humanity by his sceptical pessimism, his denial of man's virtue and heroism.

[2] It is noticeable that after this, the playful detachment, the indulgent irony disappears from Conrad's writing altogether.

Lena, the vitality, trust and energy springing from the very depths of degradation. The reader is not allowed to forget Lena's origins: her accent betrays them in every sentence. Together, Heyst and Lena symbolise all that Conrad approved of—the power of rectitude and the power of love. They stand for humanity at large, betrayed to evil, but uncorrupted, and in pathos and dignity their fate cannot be matched in all Conrad's work.

III. RECOLLECTIONS IN
TRANQUILLITY

WITH the completion of *Victory* Conrad's main work
was ended. In *Lord Jim* he had started on the
exploration of fidelity and betrayal, the survey of the
moral world. He had followed the advice of his own
Stein: "In the destructive element immerse."[1] The
ranging scope of *Nostromo*, the narrowed concentra-
tion of the two political novels, the analytic probings
of *Chance* and the aphoristic firmness of *Victory* had
completed the survey so begun. Conrad's later novels
are for the most part sound, careful, but incurably
listless works. They are exercises in the manner of
Conrad.

There are only five books in these ten years, for the
posthumous volume, *Tales of Hearsay*, consists mostly
of old uncollected stories. These five books are
reminiscent of Conrad's youth, in a direct, simple
way. It has been said that he often repeated characters and incidents: thus besides Marlow, Almayer
and Lingard, Schomberg also appears in *Lord Jim*,

[1] *Lord Jim*, p. 214. "He wants to be a saint and he wants to
be a devil—and every time he shuts his eyes he sees himself
as a very fine fellow—so fine as he never can be....A man
that is born falls into a dream like a man who falls into the
sea....So if you ask me—how to be?...In the destructive
element immerse. That was the way. To follow the dream,
and again to follow the dream—and so—*ewig—usque ad
finem....*"

Falk and *Victory,* Hollis in *Karain* and *Because of the Dollars,* the suicide captain in *Falk* and *The Shadow Line,* Davidson of the *Sissie* in *Almayer's Folly, Victory* and *Because of the Dollars.* Of Conrad's living models, Dominic Cervoni occurs four times at least,[1] besides appearing in his own person in *The Mirror of the Sea.* Conrad's memory was amazing. He could remember for years some momentary contact, such as that with the girl who stood for Lena. In his last years, freed from worldly anxiety but tormented by illness and the war of 1914–18, Conrad drew more and more on pure reminiscence. *The Shadow Line,* for instance, is a return to "sea-stuff", but it reads like a very clever imitation of the early Conrad. Everything is there—the command of phrasing, the thumb-nail character sketches, the great seascapes—everything except verve, the informing spirit which made the old tales live. *The Arrow of Gold* is a straightforward recollection of Conrad's early days at Marseilles and of his first love, a subject which cut so deep that he had never attempted it before. He does not succeed here. The facts are there, of course, and one or two passages have some life; but the very writing is for the most part turgid and clogged:

She listened to me, unreadable, unmoved, narrowed eyes, closed lips, slightly flushed face, as if carved six thousand years ago in order to fix for ever the something

[1] In *Nostromo, The Arrow of Gold, The Rover* and *Suspense.*

secret and obscure which is in all women. Not the gross immobility of a Sphinx proposing roadside riddles, but the finer immobility, almost sacred, of a fateful figure seated at the very source of the passions that have moved men from the dawn of ages.

(The Arrow of Gold, pp. 145–6)

The only comment on this which seems possible is that of the Carpenter: "The butter's spread too thick!"

The Rescue is an even clearer and sadder case. It is the story of a betrayal—like *Karain, The Lagoon,* and *Lord Jim.* But the pressure of pity and fear, the sense of the trap and the struggle are hardly there at all. Mrs Travers is the most conventional of *femmes fatales,* completely equipped down to a pair of dewy violet eyes. Her husband is meant to be of a sinister and hardhearted triviality—like a much deteriorated version of Charles Gould mixed with Mr Vladimir. As for Lingard, the bewitched, the willing prey, he comes to life least of all.[1]

There would be no point in dwelling on such unfortunate examples of encroaching senility, were it not that they place in stronger relief the last

---

[1] "He was like a blind force. She closed her eyes altogether. Her head fell back a little. Not instinctively, but as it were with wilful resignation, and from a sense of justice she abandoned herself to his arms" (p. 395). "'Hate. Love. What can touch you? For me you stand above death itself, for I see now that as long as I live you will never die'" (p. 465). These passages are typical.

success, *The Rover*. This book was thrown off suddenly, a by-product of the long unfinished novel,
Suspense. It appeared spontaneously, as *The Nigger
of the Narcissus* had done in 1897: and it was quickly
written, like *Youth* and *The Heart of Darkness*.
Suspense itself is rambling: Mrs Conrad declared that
Conrad intended to prune it drastically. But *The
Rover* is brief.[1] The story is lurid, yet it is kept at a
delicate remove from the reader, so that the effect
is one of airy heroism, of a melodramatic idyll. The
temper is that of Shakespeare's final period; from
a point beyond his tragedies, Conrad is playing, not
frivolously, but elusively, with his own tragic themes.

The Rover, old Peyrol, revives Dominic Cervoni
of the *Tremolino*: and Arlette and Eugène Réal are
the last examples of Conrad's frustrated lovers. They
are more bitterly repressed than any of the others;
in Réal, the son of a "ci-devant", it is possible that
Conrad is drawing his own shell-shocked son. It is
old Peyrol alone who can penetrate the sombre self-
sufficiency of the naval lieutenant.

He was, of course, very self-contained. Peyrol, whom
he had found unexpectedly settled on the peninsula, was
the first human being to break through that schooled
reserve which the precariousness of all things had forced
on the orphan of the Revolution.   (*The Rover*, p. 71)

[1] "Perhaps my only work in which brevity was a conscious
aim. I don't mean compression, I mean brevity *ab initio*..."
(*Life and Letters*, vol. II, p. 326).

But even Peyrol does no more than elicit confidences:
he cannot revive the feeling of life in Réal.

> ...Réal leaned his back against the wall, and folded
> his arms in the familiar way of their talks.
> "Ennui, Peyrol", he said, in a far-away tone.
> "Confounded boredom."
> Peyrol also, as if unable to resist the force of example,
> assumed the same attitude, and said:
> "You seem to be a man that makes no friends."
> "True, Peyrol. I think I am that sort of man."
> "What, no friends at all? Not even a little friend of
> any sort?"
> Lieutenant Réal leaned the back of his head against
> the wall, and made no answer.
> (*The Rover*, p. 205)

Arlette's life had been one not of privation but of
horror. She had been caught up in the Massacres at
Marseilles when quite a child, and forced to run with
the mob—to carry a woman's head on a pike—to live
a maniacal life. She comes back to the farm at
Escampobar shocked into insensibility, light as a
ghost and almost as vacant. Réal fears that he has
fallen in love with "body without mind". It is part
of his torment that Arlette appears to be only a lovely
shell, as so many of Conrad's women are. Only at
the end does he realise, like Heyst, that "she, whose
little feet had run ankle deep through the terror of
death, had brought to him the sense of triumphant
life" (*The Rover*, p. 260). The love which springs
between the two has at first only the anguish of life

returning to the numbed minds, and on Réal's part, since he is engaged on a naval mission which involves certain capture by the English, there is an overwhelming sense of guilt.

"I laughed because I thought of all the days to come. Days and days and days. Have you thought of them?"

"Yes", Réal faltered, like a man stabbed to the heart, holding the door half open. And he was glad to have something to hold on to.

...He had the strength of mind to shut the door after. ...The room became dark suddenly. He thought "A cloud over the moon, a cloud over the moon, an enormous cloud" whilst he walked rigidly to the window, insecure and swaying, as if on a tight rope. After a moment he perceived the moon in a sky on which there was no sign of the smallest cloud.

(*The Rover*, pp. 223–4)

The choice confronting Réal is that which confronted all the earlier heroes; unlike them all, he goes on his mission. But Arlette, shocked back into life by her love, flies down to the little *tartane* in which Réal is to sail:[1] and by a stratagem, Peyrol gets the lieutenant

[1] It is interesting to notice that at this moment of returning life, Arlette is described in a simile identical with that used of Flora in a similar situation: the image of drowning. "The lieutenant, his bare head dripping with rain water, looked as if he had just saved her from drowning....Arlette's hair was hanging far below the lieutenant's arm in an inert and heavy mass" (p. 249). It is also interesting that Réal, like the man who acts as the voice of conscience in *Lord Jim*, is a French naval lieutenant, and that in Peyrol Conrad has combined a self-portrait with a portrait of his hero Dominic Cervoni.

ashore and goes in his place, like another Sidney
Carton, to "plant" the forged dispatches on Captain
Vincent, at the cost of his own life.

Peyrol, Captain Vincent and the seamen of the
Amelia, even Lord Nelson himself, appear as glori-
fications of the "sea-stuff". Conrad wrote no finer
passage of sea-stuff than the chase of the *tartane*
by the *Amelia*. The death of Peyrol is undimmed
heroism, and his peasant boatman Michel is the
apotheosis of all the patient humble figures in the
background of Conrad's stories, and sums up for all
of them in a phrase which touches the heart but
not the emotions, exactly as Conrad would desire.
As they sail, Peyrol says:

"Doesn't it seem funny to you, as you look back at the
shore, to think that you have left nothing and nobody
behind?"

Michel assumed the attitude of a man confronted by
an intellectual problem. Since he had become Peyrol's
henchman he had lost the habit of thinking altogether.
Directions and orders were easy things to apprehend:
but a conversation with him whom he called "notre
maître" was a serious matter demanding great and
concentrated attention. . . . He connected Peyrol's words
with his sense of his own insignificant position at the tail
of all mankind: and, timidly, he murmured with his
clear, innocent glance unclouded, the fundamental axiom
of his philosophy:

"Somebody must be last in this world."

(*The Rover*, pp. 252–3)

The rarefied clarity of the writing, the play of humour and pity and affection, is truly Shakespearean. In Conrad's *Tempest* the Ferdinand and Miranda of his rocky coast are enchanted only by the strange powers in the depths of their own minds: and Peyrol, their Prospero, releases them by the force of his simple vitality. It is the supreme case of the simple coming to the rescue of the complex. All three characters recall his earlier work: but in Michel he has embodied something which was only suggested in the crews of the *Narcissus* and the *Nan Shan*. The subtle characters are here reduced to comparative simplicity by their strange fates, but the simpler characters brought to such elemental integrity that they have the direct and plangent effect of some musical note echoing on the rock-bound, bare and brilliant shores of Provence.

Dr Gustaf Morf has seen in *The Rover* the solution of all Conrad's mental conflicts. Indeed it erupted so suddenly in his mind, like an island thrown up from some submarine volcano, that the origin must have been deepseated. In Dr Morf's words, "The writing of *The Rover* marked a turning point in his mental development. It is the first of his books in which the outcast gets back to his country, and what is still more significative, in which he proves beyond doubt that he is, in spite of everything, a good patriot...with an eloquence which stands in strange contrast to the reticence of *A Personal Record* and *Poland Revisited*."[1]

A mind at once so passionate and so distrustful of passion could not have expressed itself in any other way. *A Personal Record* is the account of how Conrad came to write in the English language—it is not, and it is not meant to be, anything but a logbook of his progress. In the "Familiar Preface" he expressly repudiates any other intention. In *Poland Revisited* he gives the dry account of which the living emotions are recreated for Peyrol, the same age as Conrad, when he returned from exile with riches of foreign lands. Conrad could never speak out except in terms of his art. It was the condition of his achievement. "The more perfect the artist, the more completely separate in him will be the man who suffers and the mind which creates."[2]

*　　*　　*　　*

Conrad's work is relevant to-day because it was produced in that simpler Europe which existed before 1914; it was written in the presence of general standards of public sanity to which we never returned in the post-war years. Yet by the peculiar history of his country, his family, and himself, Conrad knew horrors almost equal with those of to-day; and in this

[1] Gustaf Morf, *The Polish Heritage of Joseph Conrad* (Sampson Low, 1930), pp. 201, 222.
[2] T. S. Eliot, *Selected Essays* (Faber and Faber, 1931), p. 18: "Tradition and the Individual Talent."

particularly commanding position he was fitted to be an example of a "good European"—a type which belongs not to the past but the future. In himself, he knew and loved Poland, France and England: he loved England most proudly, France most warmly, Poland most deeply. His reconciliation of their conflicting claims, and his sympathy with the best of what was common to the three, is his final triumph of reducing the complex to the simple, and the one which deserves the gratitude of all.

BOOKS ON CONRAD

A SELECT LIST

BIOGRAPHICAL

Life and Letters of Joseph Conrad, ed. G. Jean-Aubry. 2 vols. Heinemann, 1927.

Joseph Conrad as I knew him. By Jessie Conrad. Heinemann, 1926.

The Last Twelve Years of Joseph Conrad. By Richard Curle. Sampson Low, 1928.

BIBLIOGRAPHICAL

A Conrad Library.... Collected by T. J. Wise. Privately printed, London, 1928.

A Conrad Memorial Library. The Collection of G. T. Keating. Doubleday, Doran and Co. New York, 1929.

A Check List of Additions to a Conrad Memorial Library, 1929–1938. By J. T. Babb. (Yale University Library Gazette, 1938, vol. XII, pp. 30–40.)

CRITICAL

A. *Books*

Gustaf Morf. *The Polish Heritage of Joseph Conrad*. Sampson Low, 1930. (A psychological study of the works in the light of Conrad's history.)

R. L. Mégroz. *Joseph Conrad's Mind and Method*. Faber and Faber, 1931. (The best critical introduction. Contains also chronological lists of works, and a bibliography for the general student.)

Edward Crankshaw. *Joseph Conrad, Some aspects of the art of the novel*. John Lane, The Bodley Head, 1936. (A stimulating but rather difficult study. Contains acute criticism of Conrad, but should not be read at an early stage.)

B. *Essays*

Henry James. *Notes on Novelists*. Dent, 1914. "The New Novel."

Virginia Woolf. *The Common Reader, First Series*. Hogarth Press, 1925. "Joseph Conrad."

E. M. Forster. *Abinger Harvest*. Edward Arnold, 1936. "Joseph Conrad, a note."

INDEX

Printed in the United States
By Bookmasters